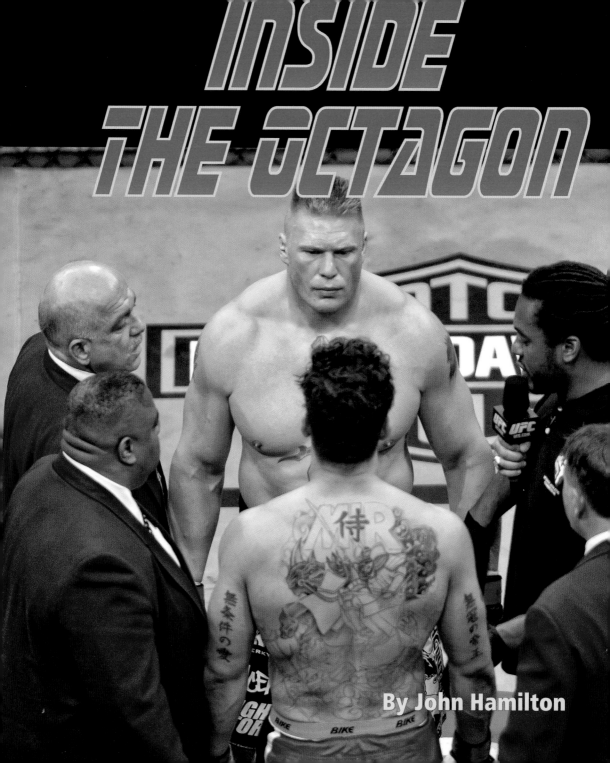

INSIDE
THE OCTAGON

By John Hamilton

Published by ABDO Publishing Company, 8000 West 78th Street, Suite
310, Edina, MN 55439. Copyright ©2011 by Abdo Consulting Group, Inc.
International copyrights reserved in all countries. No part of this book may
be reproduced in any form without written permission from the publisher.
A&D Xtreme™ is a trademark and logo of ABDO Publishing Company.

Printed in the United States of America, North Mankato, Minnesota.
052010
092010

Editor: Sue Hamilton
Graphic Design: John Hamilton
Cover Photo: AP Images
Interior Photos: AP Images, p. 2, 11 (bottom right), 22 (inset), 30-31;
Getty Images, p. 11 (top right), 19 (insets), 20-21, 24-25, 26-27, 28, 29, 32;
Ray Kasprowicz, p. 1, 3, 4-5, 6-7, 8-9, 10, 11 (top and bottom left), 12-13, 14-15, 16
(inset), 16-17, 18-19, 22-23.

Library of Congress Cataloging-in-Publication Data

Hamilton, John, 1959-
  Inside the octagon / John Hamilton.
      p. cm. -- (Xtreme ufc)
  Includes index.
  ISBN 978-1-61613-476-1
  1. Mixed martial arts--Juvenile literature. 2. Ultimate Fighting Championship
(Organization)--Juvenile literature. I. Title.
  GV1102.7.M59H37 2011
  796.815--dc22
                        2010018757

CONTENTS

ULTIMATE

The Ultimate Fighting Championship (UFC) is one of the most popular and fastest-growing sports organizations in the world. It is a mixed martial arts (MMA) competition that is intense and full of action.

Lyoto Machida

FIGHTING

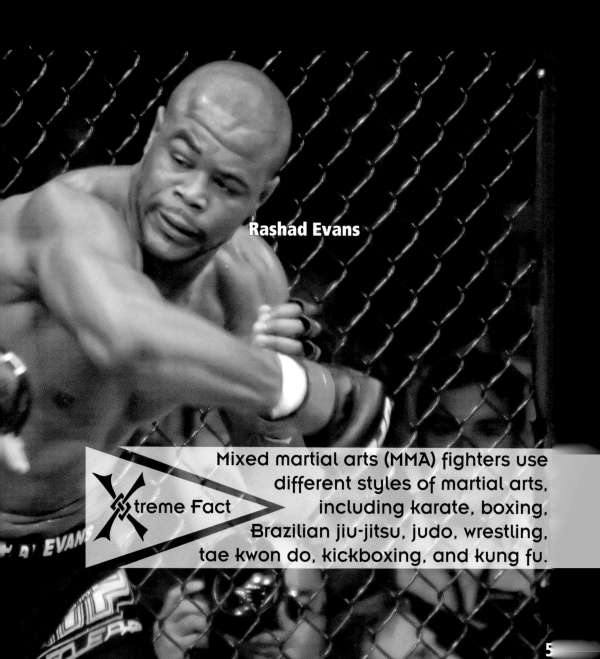

Rashad Evans

OCTAGON

UFC fighters compete in an arena called the Octagon. It is a mat and cage with eight sides. The sides are made of a metal chain-link fence with a black vinyl coating. Foam padding rests on top of the fence and between the straight sections.

30 feet (9 m)

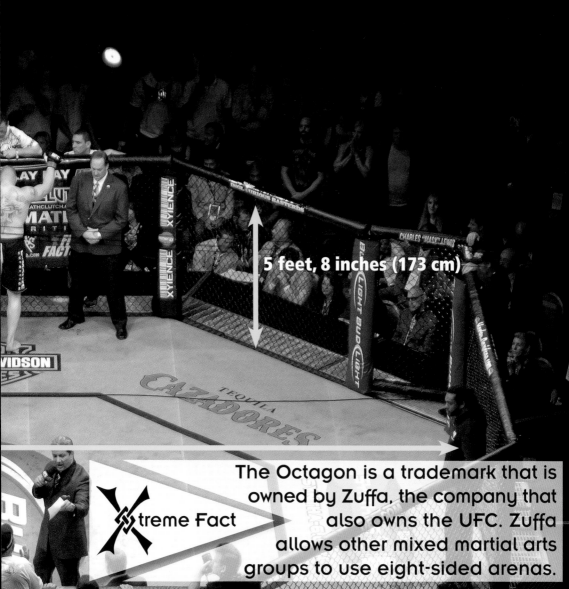

5 feet, 8 inches (173 cm)

Xtreme Fact

The Octagon is a trademark that is owned by Zuffa, the company that also owns the UFC. Zuffa allows other mixed martial arts groups to use eight-sided arenas.

Fight Rounds

UFC fights are divided into rounds. Each round is five minutes long. Most fights are scheduled to last three rounds. Championship bouts are scheduled to last five rounds. There is a one-minute rest between rounds.

Mark Coleman

Stephan Bonnar

At UFC 100 on July 11, 2009, light heavyweights Mark Coleman (top) Xtreme Fight and Stephan Bonnar fought all three rounds for 15 minutes of grueling action. Coleman won the fight.

Weight Divisions

In the early days of the UFC, there were no weight divisions. Huge sumo wrestlers could fight skinny boxers. When mixed martial arts became more popular in the late 1990s, fighters were grouped into five weight classes, similar to professional boxing. Weight divisions make the fights more fair.

Brock Lesnar
265 pounds
(120 kg)

Heavyweight
206 to 265 pounds
(93 to 120 kg)

Forrest Griffin
205 pounds
(93 kg)

**Light Heavyweight
186 to 205 pounds
(84 to 93 kg)**

Anderson Silva
185 pounds
(84 kg)

**Middleweight
171 to 185 pounds
(78 to 84 kg)**

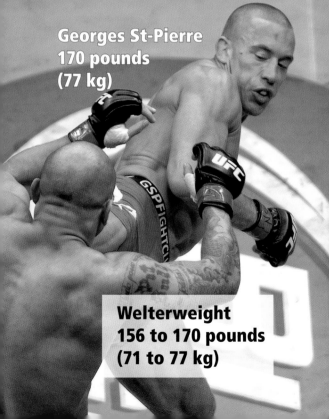

Georges St-Pierre
170 pounds
(77 kg)

**Welterweight
156 to 170 pounds
(71 to 77 kg)**

Sean Sherk
155 pounds
(70 kg)

**Lightweight
146 to 155 pounds
(66 to 70 kg)**

Tito Ortiz

Xtreme Fight
On November 21, 2009, Tito Ortiz (left) and Forrest Griffin fought at UFC 106. Known for their striking skills, they both made good use of their gloves. Griffin won the match.

Forrest Griffin

Clothes and Equipment

All UFC fighters must wear approved shorts, with no shoes. Fighters wear open-fingered gloves, with about one inch (2.5 cm) of padding around the knuckles. The gloves protect the hands from injury, but still allow fighters to grab their opponents.

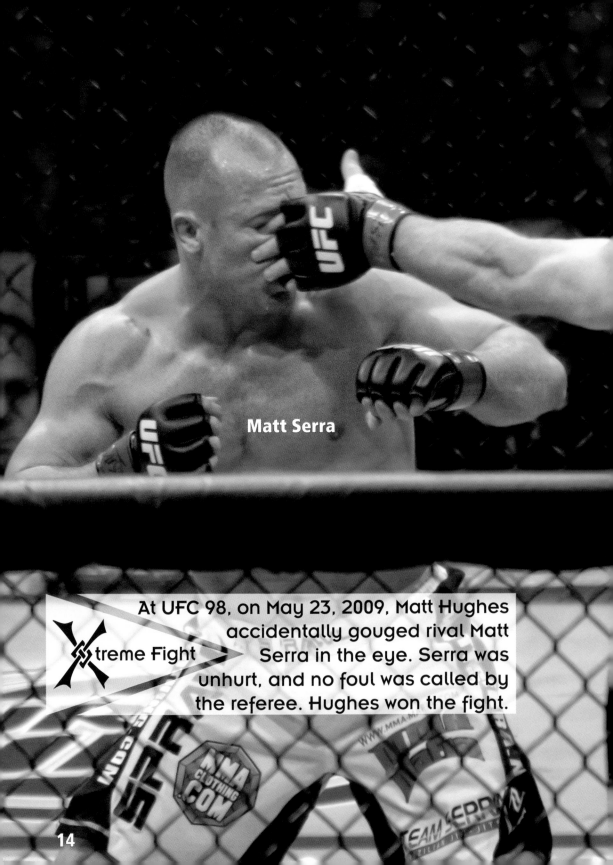

Matt Serra

At UFC 98, on May 23, 2009, Matt Hughes accidentally gouged rival Matt Serra in the eye. Serra was unhurt, and no foul was called by the referee. Hughes won the fight.

Xtreme Fight

Fouls

Matt Hughes

If the referee calls a foul, the fighter may be penalized points, or even disqualified if the foul was intentional. Fouls not allowed in the UFC include:

- eye gouging
- groin strikes
- biting
- throat strikes
- hair pulling
- kicking the head of a downed opponent.

The UFC began in 1993. Its goal was to find out which martial art was the best. After hundreds of matches, the answer is clear. Fighters who win the most are mixed martial artists. They blend many different styles and techniques.

Lyoto Machida

Brock Lesnar

Frank Mir

STYLES

Rashad Evans

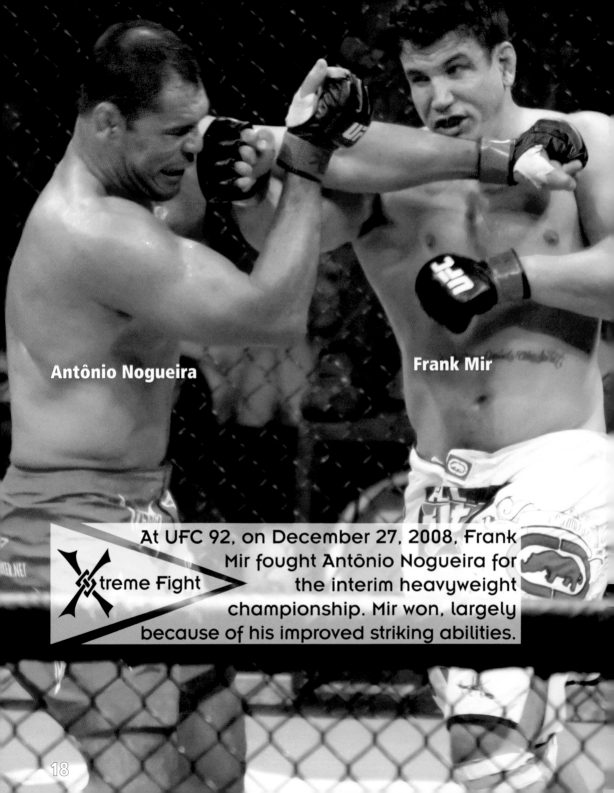

Antônio Nogueira

Frank Mir

At UFC 92, on December 27, 2008, Frank Mir fought Antônio Nogueira for the interim heavyweight championship. Mir won, largely because of his improved striking abilities.

Xtreme Fight

Punching

Striking with the fists is one of the most basic tools in mixed martial arts. A powerful punch can end a match quickly. Punches, jabs, and uppercuts are all used by skilled strikers. Elbows and knees are also used to strike. Martial arts that rely heavily on striking include boxing, karate, Brazilian jiu-jitsu, and tae kwon do.

Rashad Evans

Chuck Liddell

Keith Jardine

Ryan Bader

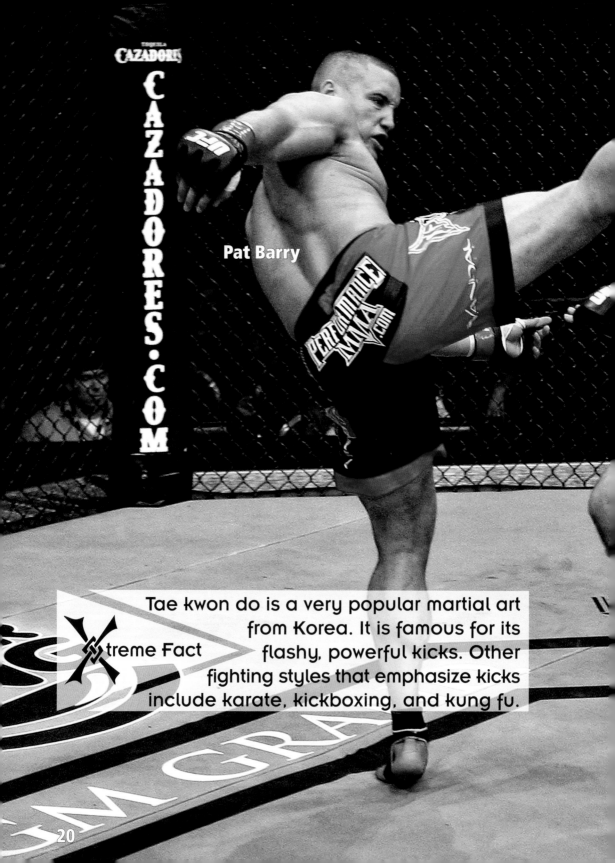

Pat Barry

Xtreme Fact

Tae kwon do is a very popular martial art from Korea. It is famous for its flashy, powerful kicks. Other fighting styles that emphasize kicks include karate, kickboxing, and kung fu.

Tim Hague

Kicking

Powerful kicks are a hallmark of the martial arts. In the UFC, skilled kickers can have a huge advantage. Knockout kicks can be thrown from a long distance, making them difficult to defend against. Kickers who also have good grappling skills make dangerous opponents.

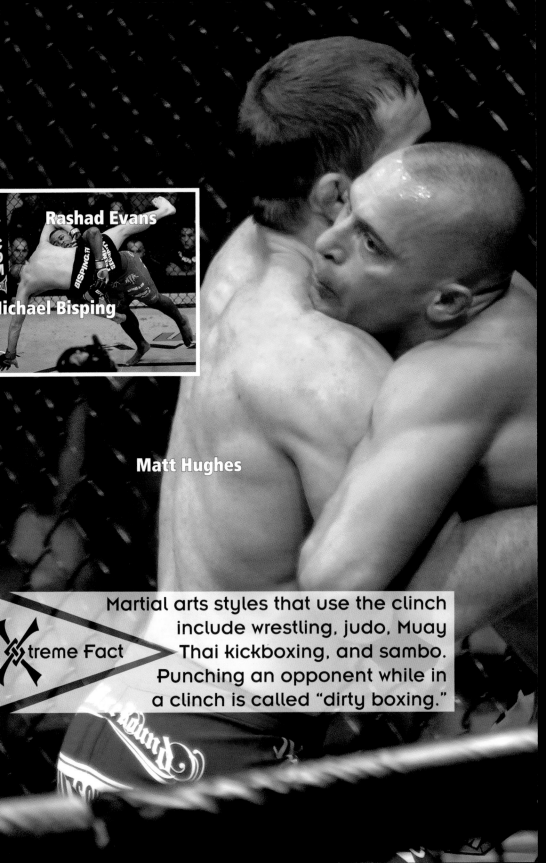

Rashad Evans

Michael Bisping

Matt Hughes

Martial arts styles that use the clinch include wrestling, judo, Muay Thai kickboxing, and sambo. Punching an opponent while in a clinch is called "dirty boxing."

Matt Serra

Clinch Fighting

Clinch fighters like to grapple their opponents, holding them tight while striking at close range. This eliminates the opponents' chance to strike. Clinch fighters also perform throws and leg sweeps, taking their opponents to the mat.

Georges St-Pierre

Thiago Alves

Welterweights Georges St-Pierre (top) and Thiago Alves battled at UFC 100, on July 11, 2009. Both fighters are Brazilian jiu-jitsu experts. St-Pierre won the match after five rounds.

Xtreme Fight

Ground Fighting

Many mixed martial artists are best when fighting on the ground. Brazilian jiu-jitsu and wrestling both emphasize ground control and positioning. Cardio conditioning is extremely important for mixed martial artists who specialize in ground fighting.

Submission Holds

Submission holds force an opponent to give up, or "submit." They include chokeholds, compression locks, and joint locks. These holds can cause severe pain or injury if sustained. Fighters signal to the referee that they submit by "tapping out," rapidly slapping the mat or their opponent's body.

Alan Belcher

Patrick Côté

Xtreme Fight

At UFC 113, on May 8, 2010, middleweight Alan Belcher (bottom) defeated Patrick Côté by putting him in a submission hold called a "rear naked choke." Côté tapped out.

WINNING

UFC fights usually end in one
of four ways:

- Knockout—When a fighter
  is knocked unconscious
  by a legal strike.
- Technical Knockout
  (TKO)—When the referee
  decides a fighter can no longer defend
  himself and stops the fight.
- Submission—When a fighter gives up by
  tapping the mat or the other fighter.
- Judges" Decision—If a fight "goes the
  distance" for all scheduled rounds, a
  panel of three judges decides the winner
  of the match.

Brock Lesnar

Heath Herring

FIGHTS

As of June 2010, middleweight Anderson Silva has the longest winning streak in UFC history, with 11 consecutive wins. Some think he is the best fighter to ever enter the Octagon.

Xtreme Fight

Brazilian Jiu-Jitsu

A fighting style made popular by fighters from Brazil that specializes in grappling and ground fighting, including chokes and submission holds.

Compression Lock

A kind of submission hold that presses muscle into bone, causing pain.

Decision

If a match finishes without a clear victor, either by knockout or submission, a panel of three judges decides the winner. If only two judges agree on the winner, it is called a split decision.

Joint Lock

A kind of submission hold that isolates and forces an opponent's joint at or just beyond its normal range of motion, causing pain. Elbows, shoulders, wrists, knees and ankles are common targets of joint locks.

GLOSSARY

Kickboxing
A style of fighting that relies mainly on a mix of kicking and punching. Muay Thai is a type of kickboxing that is the national sport of Thailand.

Mixed Martial Arts
A full-contact sport that allows a mix of different martial arts, such as boxing, karate, and wrestling. The most popular mixed martial arts (MMA) organization is the Ultimate Fighting Championship (UFC).

Octagon
The eight-sided ring in which Ultimate Fighting Championship fighters compete.

Tae Kwon Do
A martial art that is the national sport of South Korea. Tae Kwon Do emphasizes powerful strikes, especially high, leaping kicks.

INDEX